The Inner Life of Comics

Poems

Paul Juhasz

Book and Cover Design: Rowan Kehn
ISBN: 978-1-7355762-7-5

Turning Plow Press

Praise for *The Inner Life of Comics*

What do Pagliacci, Shakespeare, Coltrane, and Thoreau have in common? Paul Juhasz knows. In *The Inner Life of Comics* he unravels the tangled knot of moving through the world as a thinking, feeling man. Like Shakespeare and Thoreau, his language is layered and profound. Like Pagliacci, he is a court jester, a truth teller always among the crowd but rarely of it. And, like Coltrane's music, his minor-key bebop finds a way to your heart.

> Jeanetta Calhoun Mish
> 2017-2020 Oklahoma State Poet Laureate

There is a bone-deep weariness to this new collection of poems by Paul Juhasz. It's the weariness we've all survived after a year and more of isolation during the pandemic, but Paul's is deeper, his borne of a life fractured in middle age, of love found, then lost, of endings and new, tentative beginnings. There is also something I think of as classic Paul humor, an ability to face the worst that life throws at you and make a joke of it. Stare the hangman down, then make him laugh, right before he pulls the lever. But there's more. Though darkness, "the bear," always lurks (source, Paul reveals to us, of all great comedy), he has discovered in this collection something much finer than that, the mysterious thing we call poetry. There are lines in these poems, prose and lineated, of surpassing beauty. There are moments in these lines, in these poems, when the comic rests and the poet takes over, and we find ourselves mesmerized and lifted into a kind of peace that lets us know Paul has travelled through the darkness and come out on the other side full of truths and beauties that sustain long after the laughter fades.

> Hank Jones
> author of *Too Late for Manly Hands*

For Tim Bradford,
who showed me the way.

"Dear Mr. Fantasy play us a tune
Something to make us all happy."
Traffic

Table of Contents

Horizon

All stories are really just one story, the story of the horizon,
how we race to it, how we foolishly believe we'll get there,
rest easy, all our efforts rewarded, all our dreams silk-
screened onto posters.

Carrion birds fly back and forth, from there to here, try to
warn us off this foolishness, sing to us of the Horizon as it is:

At the Horizon, the cleric has no need for aftershave.

At the Horizon, there's a rabbit; dangling from its belt a
human foot it rubs for luck.

At the Horizon, the mulberry bush dances around us in the
fading light of a cold and frosty morning.

At the Horizon, the battered and foot-sore conquistador sits
on a mesa rim, writing on a postcard, "Wish you were here,"
in perfect, precise calligraphy.

We pay no heed, ignore the telegrams that drip from their
gore-stained beaks, ride off into the sunset anyway, chasing
tropes, McCarthy's evening redness in the west staining our
stuffed shirts.

For there, at that shimmering, elusive edge, is where the story
of the world, the one story that is all stories, remains untold,
withheld.

A something we must believe is worth catching, a story we
must believe is worth telling.

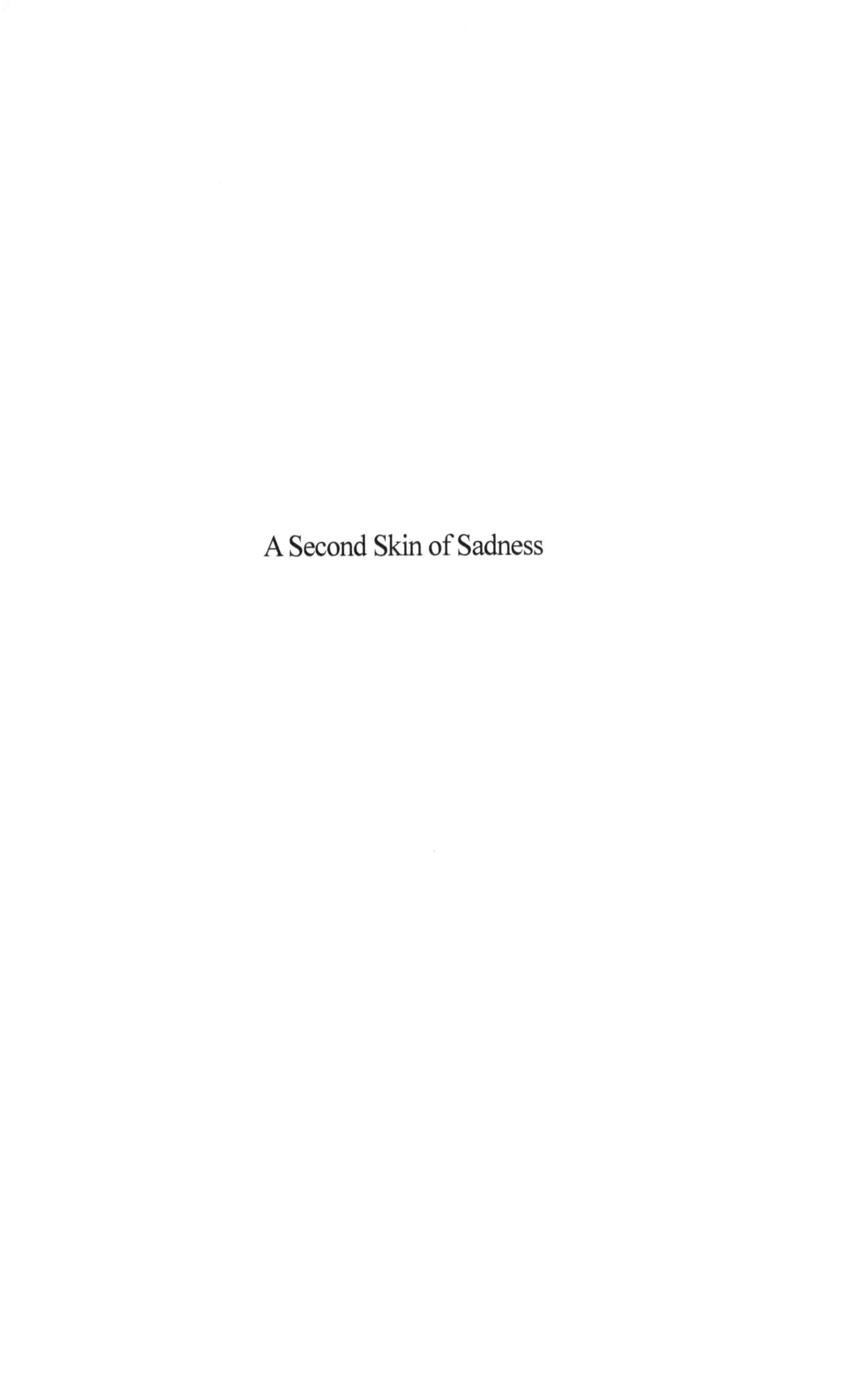

A Second Skin of Sadness

Pagliacci

"La commedia è finite!"

It's an old story, told many times, different ways. Rorschach tells it in *Watchmen*. There's an older version where the clown's name is Grimaldi. And of course, there is the original source, the Italian opera; Canio, the tragically-jealous murderer hiding under the garb of the clown. The story goes something like this: A man goes to the doctor and speaks of bottomless depression, of a second skin of sadness, of complete and utter despair. The doctor tells him the cure is simple: he should go see the famous clown, Pagliacci; that laughter will cure the depression. The man breaks down sobbing, is inconsolable. And then, the punchline: "But, Doctor, I am Pagliacci."

Interesting word: punchline. The thing that makes us laugh gilded in the language of pain. That seems to be our way. We laugh at the horrors, because the only other option—for we long ago ran out of other ideas—is to cry at them, and that simply won't do. Tears cause our make-up to run, lubricates the mask, creates slippage, the threat of sliding; makes our faces awful to look at.

But in the tears of the clown, we can still find much to laugh at. There is mirth there in the shimmering, the bastard orphan of light refracted, the promise of something eternal that only seems eternal because it is purchased by someone else. Even as he cries, to us, his face is still painted; to us, he is still dressed in motley; to us, he is still and always, just a clown.

To the Passenger with the Mirror Sunglasses in the Back Seat of the Extended Cab Pick-up Truck: A Prose Ode

Whether you're surly over forgetting to call "shotgun," or just perpetually chapped over being the least important member of the triumvirate, you carry off your proscribed duties with aplomb, glaring with reflective eyeless eyes at each passing car in turn, making us wonder if we have violated some slight rule of driving etiquette or some minor traffic law.

Our passing presence an affront to your world, you leave us with a lingering sense of guilt, an undefined awareness of obtuse transgression. Reflexive shame, thoughts of inherent corruption, of moral turpitude, linger the rest of our ride,

when, in all probability, you were merely longing for our wondrous agency, our ability to drive where and when we want, unfettered by the whims of others, never straining to comprehend partially-heard conversations, never an after-thought inclusion, a state of motion which we all too often take for granted.

Myopia

My father tells the story often. About when he was on a river cruise in Minneapolis and noticed a man climbing over the guardrail on a bridge above the Mississippi. As the man lowered himself onto a ledge and took one last wistful look around, my father called out, "Oh, c'mon. Things aren't *that* bad."

He laughs when he's done with the telling, thinking his joke is the kernel of the story, because he can only see the river's width, never its depth, never its length.

Postmortem

In hindsight, I should have known
when she jerked her head away,
trapezius stretched taut
like galvanized cable.

She had no interest
in the video I wanted to share with her,
Rage Against the Machine's
cover of "The Ghost of Tom Joad."

It wasn't about the music,
a reaction to Tom Morello's unworldly guitar playing,
or de la Rocha's abrasive lyrics,
nor was it a preference for the more restrained
indignation of Springsteen.

Either of those could have
been worked around,
part of the kaleidoscope
of likes and dislikes that make up
a shared life.

Her recoil, her refusal to immerse,
was about the video's images:
Brutal scenes of inhumanity,
of arbitrary power, codified injustice,
scenes devoid of empathy or compassion,
scenes of things one *must* look at, *must* see,
scenes of things she, steadfast,
was unwilling to acknowledge,
no matter the soundtrack.

Coltrane

I sit on a balcony,
a cup of coffee held for warmth
on a chill spring morning,
as waxwings and vireos flit and flash,
percolating with song.

Earbuds dam back the world
with Coltrane's "Alabama,"
while in the room behind the
sliding glass door, the news speaks
of Ahmaud Arbery.

Coltrane's sax melts mournful,
keeping the bass and percussion
percolating in the background at bay;
desperation and defiance blend on the reed,
build, expand, become manic,
pressing back against the growling chaos of the bassline,
before collapsing, weary and spent,
one final wail into the darkness, then
Coltrane's liquid gold tapers,
a final, lingering note fading
into full silence.

Addie Mae Collins, Cynthia Wesley, Carole Robertson
would be sixty-nine-years old now.
Carol Denise McNair would be sixty-six.

Trayvon Martin would have been twenty-five,
Eric Garner would be forty-nine,
Sandra Bland thirty-three.
Ahmaud Arbery will never be twenty-six.

I sit on a balcony
and think about a treadmill world,
where even the warbling of birds
cannot hold back the darkness
of a world stuck on repeat.

And Now, A Word from Our Sponsors

During the commercial break, twenty-six people died.

During the commercial break, a president checked his press
conference ratings with masturbatory self-absorption.

Someone planned her Spring Break, his virus-party,
indifferent to fatality rates or infection curves.

A woman wrote a grocery list she'll be too scared to use.
Every person in the aisles suspect. Are you the person who'll
kill me? Am I the person who'll kill you?

A nurse inventoried N95 masks and implications a third time.

Bus drivers, garbage collectors, drive-through window-
workers, gilded in new-found essentiality, force-offered
themselves up in our stead.

Verizon and CapitalOne announced we're all in this together,
as long as you pay your bill.

A man thought of his youngest son. They haven't spoken
since the divorce. Sometimes the father fears they've
exchanged their last words but didn't know it.

An empty orange juice bottle, blown by an Oklahoma wind,
wobble-skipped across a static parking lot. Its wind-moan, its
hollow thunk, a dirge.

A brace of deer flit across a weed-grown infield, kicking up
forgotten chalk.

During the commercial break, three minutes and thirty-five seconds elapsed.

During the commercial break, twenty-six people died.

Pandemic Coefficient

Because I need to get out.
Because I can't stay cooped up any longer.
Because I need a haircut.
Because I need to get my nails done.
Because I haven't played eighteen holes in months.
Because with all this stress, I could go for a nice massage.
Anyone for tennis?
Because it's such a nice day out.
Because Hollister and Co. is open again.
Because the kids want to go swimming
Because I've been thinking about this wicked tattoo I'm
gonna get:
        a skull and crossbones, with the caption:
        "Live Free or Die."

Support Group

Uncle Sam sits on a cold metal folding chair, his head in his hands. The famous, glowering, "I Want You" look that once so inspired replaced by a plaintive "What the fuck?" He was crying a while ago. Been a big year for crying.

"And the crying ain't over," George Floyd whispers in one ear. "Not by a long shot," the Proud Boys laugh in his other. "These symptoms shall recur if the disease remains untreated," Dr. King reminds one ear. "I'll make America great again," Donald Trump promises the other. Chief Seattle stands before him, holding a pile of frayed and weathered papers. "Is now a good time?" he asks.

Uncle Sam looks around at the rest of the support group, gathered in this circle of folding chairs, drinking tepid cups of watered-down coffee. Helen of Troy stares into her compact, blithely applying lipstick; Dr. Frankenstein is hugging himself against phantom Arctic chill, muttering in hollow confusion, "But I *created* him." Beside him, Oppenheimer mutters much the same thing. Faust, haloed in brimstone glow, ravenously reads volume after volume. Sitting next to Uncle Sam, an ordinary German from Lower Saxony sits silently, a gathering of ash powdering each shoulder. He is clouded in the faint stench of burning . . . something.

Uncle Sam stands, takes in the group with a final, dismissive glance. He is not interested in anything they have to say. He does not belong here. He is not one of them. His problem is not *that* bad. He can handle it. He is special, exceptional.

He leaves the room.

To the Driver of the Semi Hauling a Trailer from Domino's

Who the hell ordered *that* much pizza?

The Inertia of Habit

Hair grown long.
Beard to keep it company.
Clothes that make the internal me
        external now
        line my closet.
Braceleted wrists,
Necklaced neck.
Vetoed tattoos scheduled.
The hole in my ear,
        two-decades
        closed, re-pierced.
Pictures I like on walls
        where I want them.
Weekend plans whimsical
        and untethered.
Meals cooked without concern
        of allergy.

An unclipping of wings,
        a re-embrace.
Remurgence,
        unfettered,
        and individual.

But why then,
        I wonder,
        do I still shut the
        bathroom door?

Why I Became a Poet

The black line the map
promised led to the
trailhead narrowed,
more dirt than road now,
arrowed at the panhandled vistas
promised by the work-week.

Nailed to a post
scar-jammed
among cactus and scrub
a sign signified:
"Private Property.
No Trespassing."

Forced to turn the car around,
I drove away from the
blisters of mesa
now forbidden,

in full awe of
the sovereignty of words,
of the worlds they whisper,
and their power
to fuck up my plans
for a Saturday.

My Apology to Hank Jones

You asked me one night as you poured drinks in your kitchen to write a poem about a $56 bottle of wine you bought at a gas station. We laughed, toasted the poem's successful completion, and moved on to other matters. The idea of the poem lingering in the air, an assumption, a *fait accompli*.

I don't blame you, or think you were frivolously setting me up to fail. For you, who have written so powerfully about missed opportunities for manly hands, so movingly about piloting through clouds while your grounded father desperately searches for hint of your return, so comically about the intersection of Boy Scout camping trips and cats, so transcendentally about leading boys into the Buddha's belly, the idea of writing about a $56 bottle of wine you bought at a gas station probably seemed simple, a cavalier flick of wrist, the off-hand scratch of pen.

Your wife is also a masterful poet, her musings on scorpions are more enchantment than poem, transforming those prehistoric monsters into myth, into parable; her dirges mourning those lost in Vietnam, her odes to women crossing gas-station parking lots and young black men on hillsides, are soul-punching and spirit-lifting. Given her mastery, it's no surprise you would think a poem about a $56 bottle of wine you bought at a gas station could be written on command, a mere snap of the creative finger.

And it's not like I simply couldn't write a poem. Since you laid down that challenge, I've written dozens, on all kinds of subjects. I wrote one about a dead body in a road, another about an orgy, one about Coltrane's "Alabama," and one about that homeless man with the dog in Stephenville, the one the authorities ran out of town. And a whole bunch of other poems as well. Just none about a $56 bottle of wine you bought at a gas station.

It wasn't from lack of trying. I did. I really, truly did. I tried doing the whole "diamond in the rough" bit, had a piece going about how "the world will nourish in unanticipated forms, in unpredictable ways, at unexpected times," but then I decided to use that bit for a different poem, for Ron Wallace's Oklahoma anthology. Since I write prose poems, I thought about really unleashing the surreal, a hallmark of this sub-genre, and letting that $56 bottle of wine you bought at a gas station run and play in a world with hippogriffs, with tollbooths masquerading as catacombs, or townspeople transformed overnight into hermit crabs. I even thought about getting William Carlos Williams involved.

But in the end, I just had to give up. I am sorry, my friend. Perhaps when we're all together again, sharing companionship, poetry, and libation in your kitchen, something will come to me. But maybe there are some things that do not need the poet to make its magic manifest. Some things whose beauty needs no interpretation. The gift of brotherhood, for example. Or the marriage of complimentary poets. Or how we always seem able to write, even if we're not writing about the things we wanted to. And yes, one of those things is indeed the fact that you found, miraculously, a $56 bottle of wine in a gas station. It inspires me to keep looking. And when I find it, when I have first-hand knowledge of such wonderful serendipity, I promise you, Hank, *then* I will write this poem.

Most Wanted

As I stand in a long line waiting to mail a package to my sons, I find myself wandering back in my mind, in time, to the drab periwinkle post offices of my youth, and to those faces on the wall. Not just "wanted," but "most wanted." The worst men, the worst crimes. Their black and white scowls a promise ("See you in your nightmares, kid"). The world now vast and fulsome with evil.

I'm older now, and supposedly wiser. I do adult things like go to post offices. And I wonder. A lot. It helps with things like long lines, mundane errands, and regret. I wonder, for example, about our collective need to make lists. Football Top 25s, Top Movies You Need to See Before You Die, Top 5 Signs You May Have Heart Disease, or Be a Pirate. I wonder about a compulsive need to rank so great even the FBI had to get in on it, then share their list in post offices, of all places. Because drug traffickers and terrorists, I suppose, send Christmas cards, need money orders, buy stamps too.

And I wonder about the man who just missed making the list, coming in at #11. What of him? Is he disappointed? Is the list a challenge? "Hey, brother," does it say, "you better up your game. This ain't CandyLand"? Is Number 11 angry or upset? Does he track down Number 10 and off him? Or does he perhaps find comfort in his anonymity? His ability to step out of his fugitive life for a few moments, mail jars of homemade chokecherry jam to his cousin in relative safety? Does he breathe in the air of temporary normalcy, and become wistful, filling his idle time with wonder?

The line shuffles forward, bringing me one step closer to the only worker, who will apologize for the wait. I remind myself not to blame her. I also remember I need to buy stamps.

Fake News

The frog
in water
in the pot
on the stove
has no concern.

At the Edge of All We Have Known

Second Dream Poem

"Before the seven there was the four," the pedant whispers over his shoulder, his aphorisms askant. "You are number five," he adds, giving me a coat of buffalo to ward off the chill. The coat full of lice, a groovy vibe. But that Mona Lisa seems like a shady bitch, so he climbs into the Yellow Submarine, cuts through an ocean of curdled cheese and cream, the white and orange popsicles of my youth. "At least they ain't maggots," Oscar calls from his can. He might be laughing. They Might Be Giants.

"Peace in Our Time," the news hawker shouts. "I think you're burying the lede," I tell him. "My favorite fruit is a tight, young cunt. So fresh and ripe," he replies. He laughs, then begins to cry. He tells me the Great Tragedy of the Yankee Candle is that the wax has nowhere to drip. I don't know what to say to that, so I descend via umbrella to the jungle floor.

Below the tree line, the unemployed philosopher displays his wares, a line of outdated vacuum-cleaners arranged in formation. "But these all suck," I say. "Precisely," he replies. We laugh. Nothing left to do, but quote himself: "Sometimes, if you gaze long enough into the abyss, the abyss will gaze back, which is bad. But sometimes, the abyss decides you're not worth gazing at at all, which is much worse." He stumbles into the underbrush, drunk on Mr. Pibb and Mentos. He refused to shake my hand, piebald with Pop Rocks, so I shook it myself.

The ticket-taker arrives with the meal under chrome dome, a trapezoid of pressed meat she labels steak from Salisbury, where Peter Gabriel sings on his hill. I ate, as did she, as did the others, as did you; all of us silently terrified there wouldn't be enough sauce to go round. She calls all of this a fever dream; someone else called it a carnival, another a ticker-tape parade; all of us ignorant that the tickings of a watch are not a culmination, but millennia echoes of a giant heart sobbing its own absence.

In Memoriam, I-40, Mile Marker 200.8

When traffic came to a standstill west of Nashville,
when the traffic jam counter on my Waze App ascended from
29 to 72 to 98 minutes,
I at first congratulated myself on my good fortune, an
atypical good decision to stop ten minutes earlier to grab a
water, hit the bathroom, fill-up the gas tank.

Then I spent 15 minutes jamming out, first to Zeppelin's
"When the Levee Breaks" then to Nathaniel Ratcliffe and the
Night Sweats' "I Need Never Get Old" at full blast.

When I saw a truck driver get out of his cab and stretch his
legs, I joined him. We exchanged a few jokes, then I popped
my trunk, grabbed an old, tattered football I keep there to fill
unexpected moments. We tossed the ball around for about
half an hour, weaving in and out of the static stretch of
parked cars. When we noticed the cars in front begin to creep
forward, we shook hands and resumed our separate journeys
together.

You were dying not even a mile away.

By the time I crept by the crash, they had taken most of you
away from the cab of the pickup, accordioned into the back
of a semi. Nothing left except some viscera an unlucky cop
was pulling free from the asphalt with what looked like
kitchen tongs, and a single shoe.

So there was no one to whom I could apologize for my
earlier frivolity;
no one from whom to ask forgiveness;
no one to share the surprise of pulling over a few miles later,
overwhelmed with unexpected tears;

no one to share my hope that friends and family décor your
mile-marker with flowers and maybe an icon or two;
my hope that these shame-laden words, penned when I got to
my hotel hours later, will suffice until they do;
my hope that you do not begrudge me those minor vital
celebrations of life ignorantly performed in the last moments
of your own,
our respective roles based on nothing more substantial than
the vagary of ten minutes.

Ally

Dear George,

I bought a T-shirt reading "I Can't Breathe" a week after, well, you know. It didn't arrive in time for the Black Lives Matter protests, but I went anyway. I wear the shirt with regularity, sometimes even when I go out. Although when I do, I wear a grey flannel—unbuttoned, though—over it. Of course, this condenses its message to "an't Brea." One time, though, some redneck at the Walmart figured it out anyway, and boy, did he give me hell. I thought about making an analogy to "Save the Whales," how that slogan does not mean "Fuck fish, or seals, or dolphins, or walruses (walrii?)," but I don't think this mullet cared much about the life aquatic either. So I said nothing, unless we consider the shirt's message as a voice, in which case I said, "an't Brea." It was an awkward experience. Quite awful, actually. Made me anxious, because I thought the guy might possibly hit me. I tell you, my heart was racing by the time I got to the Redbox kiosk near the door (where I rented *American History X*. Man, Ed Norton is great in that).

Closing arguments were this morning. The verdict can come down any moment now. I hope, some day, I'll be brave enough to leave the grey flannel home.

~~Yours~~
~~Warmest regards~~
~~Best regards~~
Regards

~~A friend~~
~~Paul~~
An ally

He Used a Choke Collar

It was a control issue, he said. Keep it on the path. You can't have it run willy nilly, after any squirrel or rabbit that catches its eye or nose. (And yes, he used the phrase "willy nilly." Odd, I know, for a man who uses a choke collar to also use such charming anachronisms.)

He found them vital for what he called "training," and it cannot be questioned that his dog was well-behaved, meek and submissive, around him.

I'd wince every time he'd pull that chain. But he always had an explanation, a justification. And, after all, he had far more experience in such matters, so it was hard to judge or push back.

And to be fair, he never went for the choke collars with the prongs curving in, the ones that enforce the intended lesson with pin-prick precision. Needlessly cruel, he called them. He preferred the circular suffocation, slow and steady. More egalitarian. And yes, he used the phrase "egalitarian." Odd, I know, for a man who uses a choke collar to also use such charming anachronisms.

He used a choke collar. It was a natural thing for him to do. And it wasn't until long after—when I found myself for the first time in a dog park—that I saw there were so many others who didn't.

Free Association

First List
       1. Closed
       2. Awkward
       3. Laughter
       4. Transition
       5. Solitude

Second List
       1. Strip malls
       2. Concrete
       3. Empty
       4. False Start
       5. Rewind

Third List
       1. Marble Rye
       2. Cracks
       3. Laughter
       4. Weeds
       5. Kaleidoscope

Final List
       1. Bubble gum
       2. Eclipse
       3. Laughter
       4. Palimpsest
       5. Eraser

Taxonomy

I don't know the names of trees. Beyond that demarcation
between deciduous and evergreen, I got nothing. I can tell a
maple tree, but only because I've watched hockey all my life.

I don't know the names of birds, either. Or not many,
anyway. Some broad categories. Crows, hummingbirds,
doves, birds of prey. But if you were to point at a particular
bird of prey and ask me what it was, I'd probably not have
much more to offer. I *can* readily identify an ostrich if I had
to. Or a number of other flightless birds: cassowary, emu,
kiwi. But living as I do in central Oklahoma, such knowledge
is of little use.

It's not just natural things either. I don't know the names of
cars. I can identify a Nissan Murano only because I drive
one. Other than that, only if I'm close enough to read the
back bumper. I am, unintentionally, a great help to fugitives
from justice.

I don't know my own name. The one engraved into the fabric
of the Universe. I answer to "Paul" for the convenience of
others, but I don't know my own name. The one not laden
down by words like "purpose," and "knowledge." Until I do,
I'll meander, missing some guideposts, catching others, adrift
in this schematic nothingness built on more important matter
than the recitation of names.

50

When I was younger, when numbers were irrelevant, real in the academic sense only, I assumed this would be the mid-point. Neat and symmetrical. Now that I'm here, I hardly think that's the case. Not even sure I want it to be.

Such a surreal number, really. It's not that I don't feel it; that's hardly surprising. I just got here nine hours ago. It's that I seem, somehow, inappropriate, unanticipated. I'm still that young, bewildered boy, question-laden, unsure of direction and identity.

Is it too late to find a career? Is it too early to decide careers are unnecessary?
Is my first book indeed a "first"? Or an "only"?
Will there be a day when I'm no longer afraid of clowns? Is that when they pounce?
Will I see the Yellowstone again? With whom will I be sharing the view?
Will any of my poems be celebrated? Or all only tolerated?
Why do I have to get off the jungle-gym? And who are *you* to tell me to do so?
Will I feel the touch of love again? And what does it mean if I don't?
Am I too old to still chase the spirit? Am I too young to embrace the soul?
Is my long hair a new look? Or have I just given up?
Will I be remembered? Will I remember?
Will the uncertainty ever go away? And do I want it to?

How wonderful to have so many questions, at the age when I once thought I'd have all the answers.

Just a Hobby

Does the operator
of the jigsaw
that cuts the image
give any thought
to the picture that is
sundered?
To the unity shattered?
Or to the one
who must now reassemble
its fragmented pieces?

Intersection

Waiting for the light to change.
The radio station is playing
"It's the End of the World as We Know It (and I Feel Fine)".
I acknowledge the poor taste with a smile sardonic.

In my rearview,
a compromised foray to Wal-Mart
and its panic-bare shelves,

Lining the road before me,
fears of unpaid rent
and rendered sons half a country away.

I almost miss seeing him.
A sun and wind-faded camouflage coat,
blue jeans slightly less worn than he is,
gray and white hair spilling down his face
in deliquescing strands.

He holds an eternally-creased cardboard sign
that reads: "Anything Helps."

I have only three dollars cash,
my last tip before sheltering-in-place.
Three dollars.
A far cry short of the Anything
the man needs,
but I offer it to him anyway.

"I'm sorry.
That's all I have
on me."

"Brother," he replies
under hinting blue eyes
that hollowed out the world long ago,
"it's like the sign says."

Breakfast Thoughts

I always laugh
when the sausage links roll
about in the pan.

Where do they think
they're going?

Stupid sausage links.

Green World

In *Anatomy of Criticism*, Northrop Frye coins the term "Green World"—a "world of desire, not as an escape from 'reality,'" Frye explains, "but as the genuine form of the world that human life tries to imitate."

In graduate school I was asked to appreciate how Frye's concept operates in Shakespeare's plays. There is some conflict, in Athens, in Sicily, in some French duchy. Shakespeare's characters flee this trouble-laden place, relocate to an alternate Green World—a place pastoral, arboreal, natural—where the conflict is resolved and then, the characters return to the unsettled place they left.

As I walk through the towering oak and elm of the Shenandoah or amongst the bristlecone pine of the Great Basin, my understanding of this movement, this repositioning, is molecular, a feeling of puzzle-piece-completion. But still, there's something about Frye's Green World that I don't buy, that has always troubled me, an invalidating flaw that sinks the entire concept.

The Green Worlds I visit aren't idyllic, of course. Sometimes there's a large crowd of novices at the pond I hoped to have to myself; sometimes there's a rattlesnake basking across the trail; sometimes Doppler affects the silent solitude. But these are minor issues, easily avoided or addressed. And because he understood what it was to be human, Shakespeare's Green Worlds were not inconvenience-free either: Bottom was disfigured with the head of an ass. Antigonus is chased by a Bohemian bear who has, we must assume, pernicious intent; and everyone frolicking through the forests of Arden had to deal with Jaques's melancholy bitching, his "all the world's a stage" blather.

Unlike Shakespeare's characters, I do not find love out here,
I do not rediscover a Hermia; I do not become reconciled
with a Hermione. But that's not the trouble, either. While I
may lack a Rosalind, I often find loamy trails that I can walk
barefoot, kneading this soil between my toes. I often come
upon unexpected vistas, have profound thoughts whispered in
my ear by a spirit older than mine, and in many ways, these
are the same thing as love.

My issue is with the idea's back half. As I sit on a boulder,
idly tossed aside by a glacier with somewhere else to be,
when I take a deep breath of pure, untainted air, when I am
surrounded by the sounds of bird call, of leaf fall, of wind
and tree dancing together, I understand why we come here,
while at a complete loss as to why we go back.

Love in the Time of Coronavirus

How does one write a love poem for someone they haven't
met yet? Someone, now that the world is sundered, they may
never meet? Right now, she is a shadowy outline, haunting
the lakeside pathway at the local zoo, where our first kiss was
scripted.

How is she dealing with *her* loneliness?
Did she cut her hair for a different look, a different feel?
Does she also practice "Little Talks"
for a future karaoke duet?
Is she thinking about adopting a dog,
scrolling through local websites,
wondering whom to rescue?

The bed we first make love in is half cold,
a binary paused and unfulfilled.
I do not know if our vectors have been
aligned, or disrupted?
If we meet when this is over,
will we recognize each other?
Or will we walk on by,
unaware of what was missed?

This love more full of questions than substance.
Can you feel phantom pain for what you haven't lost?
How does one write a love poem for someone they haven't
met yet?

Press Conference

Nero puts down his fiddle,
looks out into the blaze,
and screams into the inferno,
"The fire's out."

Reading Yeats on New Year's Eve

The palsied light from the single bulb is just enough to make
out the words if I strain. It's cold on the balcony. Quiet, too.
Deathly quiet. Post-apocalyptic, as if the accumulated
tragedies of the year finally reached a critical mass, stifling
us all. If there were parties, they were muted and, in these
opening hours of what comes next, long-abandoned.

There was a shattering drunken break-up in the parking lot
around 9:30, the man slurring through his venomous
accusations with violent intensity, the woman sobbing sitting
on the cold asphalt after he thundered away in his car, newly
loosened upon the world. I doubt either made it to midnight.

The only other noise, as I sat in the coldness of the dying
year, in the birth of the new one just as cold, was the chime
of a door-ajar alarm, pinging from several parking lots away,
carried to me by gusts of wind like forgotten sonar, until that
too faded away, the car's battery drained dead.

After that, nothing but silence. Beside me on the patio table,
a tumbler of Old Forrester, a toast of dubious import. The
coldness of the world taunting my redundancy of ice.

The center was always fragile. We know that now. The myth
of progress dead before me, its corpse slowly buried in a
shroud of snow, falling like ash in the silence of the year's
earliest hours. What unfathomable beast slouches its way
towards us now?

January 1, 2021

Insomnia

Why are there synonyms for "unique"?

-43-

Hide Every Trace of Sadness

Everyone says the same thing when they pose me for a picture: "You can do better than that," or "No, a *real* smile," or they drag the word out like I'm an infant; "Ssssmmmmiiilllllleeee." They want smiles. They want the happy boy at Christmas. They want the loving family photo. They want the confident serenity of middle age. They want smiles that are genuine, that reassure, that confirm life is still worthwhile if you just . . .

But a smile is just a scar, its shape determined by the wound.

Extreme Unction

Here, at the intersection of
fear and justice,
I do not mourn a disrupted "normal."
I say instead, 'Let the chrysalis crack,
and the remurgence begin.'

And so,
if ever my words were cautious,
if I did not stand tall enough or firm enough,
if the visceral stayed academic,
until we saw a knee and a neck on TV,

if ever I dismissed your breath,
talked over your voice,
delayed you pardon and peace,
overlooked your essentiality,
or failed to take your hand,

if ever I caused you pain,
felt comfortable within my own privilege,
held you down with my own need,
I ask you your forgiveness
here, at the edge of all we have known.

Silent Movie Suicide

The thing that surprised me about my suicide was how quiet it was. I had long known this was coming, the day when the cigarette burns couldn't cauterize the pain anymore. But I always thought it'd be in Technicolor, an '80s action flick. Mel Gibson and his flowing locks gilding the act with swashbuckling daring-do; a blaze of glory kinda thing. My gesture applauded and understood, talked about as the credits rolled over some power ballad, or Sinatra singing "My Way."

But Mel wasn't there. Nor did Chuck Norris stop by. No Patrick Swayze, no Jan-Michael Vincent, no Steven Seagal. Even Fred fucking Ward was apparently too busy. There weren't even any explosions. I had always assumed Jerry Bruckheimer would show up at my suicide, eagerly hoping for a chance to blow shit up.

Lillian Gish was there, though. Looking achingly beautiful, as she did every time we've met. When we'd talk about prose poetry, California earthquakes, the script our lives could take; when we exchanged first kisses. She had a flower in her hair this time, because I told her I often dream of her like that. It was nice of her to remember. She didn't say anything. She just sat on my tattered and ratty couch with an inscrutable smile, slowly fading from the scene with each bottle of wine, each handful of pills.

The Three Stooges were there for a short while —well, Larry and Moe. Curly was testifying in court. A character witness for Lon Chaney, Jr. They somehow caught wind of the absurdity, the slapstick clusterfuck the attempt was becoming, an inadequate amount of prescription meds— barely more than a normal dosage, really—bolstered by Advil, Tylenol, whatever I could find (I think I even took a few Pepto-Bismol, because one doesn't want one's last moments to be diarrheic, I suppose). But when they found out there were no speaking lines, they quickly left.

So Chaplin came instead to negotiate the silence for me. He stayed for as long as he could, nodding with understanding, twisting his face in inscrutable pantomime. When the last moment came, he left with an avuncular pat, waddling off towards a horizon I had once hoped to reach.

I always thought I'd have a great last line. A real zinger. Sidney Carton saying, "It is a far, far better place I go to." Something like that. Hell, even Schwarzenegger's "You are one ugly mother-fucker" would do. But at my suicide, all the intertitles were blank.

I wait until the flame dies out, dust off my shoulders and rise from this pile of ash. I consider the passed-out figure on the cold, hard, tile floor surrounded by pools of vomit, decide to improvise, go off-script, break genre and speak into this silent movie suicide. "Good riddance," I say.

Off stage in his director's chair, Cecille B. DeMille calls out, "Cut. That's a wrap!"

There is talk of a sequel. My agent thinks I should pass, while I remain, for the moment, undecided.

An Ether of Our Own Crafting, Placidly Tornadic

Thank-You Note

What I really want, what I've wanted for some time now, is
to have someone smile reflexively when I enter the room,
who notices when I leave it, someone who in my dreams
wears a flower in her hair, someone to snuggle up against at
night, sharing warmth in the late autumn chill, to count with
me the space between the lightening flash and the thunder
clap, who always punctuates a kiss with a flick of tongue on
my upper lip, a comma promising a passion perpetual.

But the $10 gift card from P. F. Cheng's you sent is also nice.
I hear their Orange Chicken is quite good.

I appreciate the thought.

Et in Arcadia, Ego

I sit on a red rock slabbed into the shore bank and watch as
he casts into the vast pellucid before him, the reflection of
sky shimmered by ripples of bobber and bait. I have to
remind myself not to blink, a flick of eye that would erase the
slow counter-clockwise turn of the reel tauting the line, a
movement that, somehow, keeps him real, holds him in three
dimensions. The Oklahoma sun gives me back the color of
the outdoors as he casts again, as the ripples fade into
expansion, as he waits, placid as the waters he plumbs,
timeless and content in an idyll of his own creation.

People often comment on the resemblance, say he's a mini-
me. But my echoes are not yet the whispers of rumor to him.
Instead, I am a mini-him, reduced, faded, dwarfed by his
possibility. He is fifteen, all of his mistakes, his regrets, his
roads not taken, are but reflections of shadow still,
shimmered and ethereal.

So he casts into the vast pellucid before him, as I sit on a red
rock slabbed into the shore bank and watch, hopeful he
catches that for which I am no longer bold enough to try.

Memory

Seagull hovers in
Oklahoma sun.
How far away the ocean?
Wind echoes the lap
of waves, faint taste of
salt on its breath.

Unmade

There's something
about an unmade

bed, its promise
of resumption,
that the day is nothing
but an intermission before

I return to dreams

of a beauty so great
she makes constellations cry,

when time, distance,
circumstance
do not lie between us,

when we once again
sit beside, hands
and eyes held,
and discuss how we shall

fill the day.

Fellow Travelers

Near Staunton, Interstate 64 intersects with Interstate 81. For a long stretch, they travel together, simpatico. Sometimes the road is virtually empty of cars; sometimes the truck-traffic frustrates both lanes. Sometimes the views of Virginia's Appalachian spine overwhelm; sometimes the scenery stays forgettable and common. There is no way to mark which part of the road is I-64, which I-81, a synergy of asphalt that erases and blends.

After about thirty miles—hundreds of miles away from the welcoming sign that declares the state "is for lovers"—the roads split, each pursuing its own way, a separate continuation of a journey individual, on paths followed from the very beginning, towards destinations of solitary import, to be reached alone.

The Laughter Below

A child's laughter floats
from the downstairs apartment,
coloring my solitude.

It comes bundled
with the aroma of a
home-cooked meal, with
the foggy words of muffled
conversation,

reminding me that there
are still such things as community,
that all is not yet lost,
that there is still reason
for hope.

Hymn to Depression

Most days,
tears sudden
monsoon my shirt.
An atmospheric
sadness, unattributable
to any specific source.

But maybe every ninth
or tenth time
it is the beauty
of a song lyric that
gets me,

or the lasting
promise of a waning
sunset.

Sometimes it's the smile
uncertain a young
boy gives a stranger,
as he raises an unsteady
hand and waves.

For these subtle
gifts of sudden
release, I am
grateful,

for they whisper of
a still hope, outlined
in faded memory;
they tether me
for the day,

away from a
consuming darkness
that has always
felt like home.

Love Letter to Carl Sandburg

"My life has been the poem I would have writ,
But I could not both live and utter it."

Henry David Thoreau

Carl, I wish you could meet my downstairs neighbor, Fernando, and his family. They would recognize your Hungarians along the Desplaines, with their kegs of beer and accordions. I wish I could make you see their permanently-etched smiles; could make you hear the melody of their native tongue, soothing like birdsong; could convey the wondrous smell of his wife's cooking as it wafts up to my balcony. They are gracious, switch to English in my presence. Despite two years of undergraduate Spanish, all I can say is "I have a pencil." After thirteen-months, they are now well-aware of this fact, but always seem happy for me when I tell them.

Carl, I wish I could make you see the young man in the parking lot. See how every afternoon, he practices the same skateboard move, the one where the boarder flips his board, timing his return to the end of the board's spin with synchronic precision. It's a difficult move, and he hasn't gotten it right yet. But I don't have to explain to you that that's not the point, the every afternoon is. I wish I could make you hear the unsuccessful clatter of his failure, a metronome of determination, *muezzin* to persistence. I wish I could make you see the yellow streak he has dyed into his afro, a glance of sun he carries with him at all times. I wish you could see him, Carl. He is your dago shovelman.

I wish you could sit with me on my balcony, witness the blithe loveliness of summer Tuesday night drunkenness, shared, as if by tacit accord. The two West Africans tossing a football foreign to them near a smoking grill of kabob and hot dog; the three Czech students lugging a Bud Lite-laden cooler across the courtyard; the Portuguese couple holding hands and red wine on their balcony while awaiting the sunset; the jerky grace of the displaced Sudanese throwing a baseball to each other. I know that if I brought my glove over, they would throw to me. They would throw to you as well, Carl.

Your Chicago is everywhere. It is in Allentown, Pennsylvania, in Sioux Falls, South Dakota, right here in Oklahoma City. I think you knew this when you wrote Chicago. The world is much different now from the one you wrote about, but it is also very much the same. We didn't do a very good job of listening. We still pile the bodies high. Still let the grass do its work with casual unconcern. Still ask the ignorant what happiness is. Are still more concerned about cut-glass vases shaking in the dining cars of trains. But some of us still hear you, Carl. And there are many still who live out, with a reflexive natural grace, the poems you wrote.

Geometry

"There is no general agreement on the definition of a trapezoid." So I read in a textbook I'm inexplicably flipping through in a dusty, lonely aisle in a used bookstore.

Geometry is a branch of mathematics that studies measurement, properties, and the relationship of points, lines, and angles. An over-officious associate once defined geometry as "the study of properties of given elements that remain invariant under specified transformations," but no one really likes him, and we don't invite him to parties anymore.

This lack of consensus on the trapezoid troubles me. We've agreed on so much:

> That the right combination of angles creates a full
> circle.

> That two lines intersecting is beautiful, the point of
> intersection forever sanctified, even if
> the timing wasn't right.

> That parallel and perpendicular explain the same path.

> That the word "circumference" will always make us
> giggle, remembering the delightfully
> bad joke I told about the fattest knight at King
> Arthur's round table as we shared Bloody
> Mary's at the Mule.

> That the best shape is kaleidoscope.

I have long hoped that there would be elements that remain
invariant no matter the transformations, but now I learn that
there is no general agreement on the definition of a trapezoid.

I guess I will have to get used to that.

Shenandoah

General Grant's orders to General Sheridan

There's a copse of oak and elm a few miles from the Front
Royal station at the north edge of the park, a sunken valley
where the trees tower sixty-, seventy-feet tall, interlocked
branches rationing sunlight, corralling it into focused beams.
The air is cooler down here and the artificial sound of tires on
asphalt gives way to the warbling of vireo and thrush, the
bark of fox and squirrel. In spring, fawns gambol amongst
the fern; in fall, bear stockpile the plenty provided.

There's a copse of oak and elm a few miles from the Front
Royal station at the north edge of the park, palimpsest of a
wound that stubbornly refuses to heal.

The Inner Life of Comics

"You are the one who can make us all laugh
But doing that you break down in tears."

Traffic

The best role Robin Williams ever played was not in *Dead Poets Society,* or *Good Morning, Vietnam,* or *The Fisher King.* It was making us believe, all those years, that he was happy, balanced. That's the thing about funny people; they perform for us daily, perform so well, we blend the performance with the performer. They fool us into false-equivalencies. We hear of depression and think we understand what that word means. We think of the time when our mother cried all day when Elvis died, or when dogs went missing when we were young children.

We are young children still. We don't understand why someone can't "suck it up" or "get over it." Don't understand we might as well tell the cracks in the cement sidewalk to heal themselves. For us, sorrow is something fleeting, an insect that bites or stings, then flies away; a rushing river that churns as it flows, in which debris gets momentarily caught, is then dislodged and washed away. For the comic, sorrow is molecular, their river viscous and gummy. Through it, they force their way upstream, salmon-like, through this molasses-thick medium. It is the bear, not the spawning ground, they desire.

Until they meet the bear, they will make us laugh. They will make us laugh to keep the scab from flaking, exposing the raw wound that refuses to heal. They will make us laugh so we never feel like they do. They will make us laugh to keep their inside world from becoming ours.

I often think of the comics, of Robin and the others, a too-
long list that would be cliché if not for the horrible emptiness
they leave behind, an awful ability to make us miss someone
we have never met. The casual soothings of birdsong, the
trilling of humanity around me, the tethering it offers, fall
away. A cabalistic membership asserts itself, pushing aside
the lifelong lies I tell myself: that I am different; that I am
just naturally funny, that it has nothing to do with wounds or
attention or belonging. After a reflective sip of coffee or
wine or bourbon, depending on the hour, I must admit that I
too both love and dread the bear. I don't want to meet it, but
compulsively rush towards it. At least my flesh will nurture,
will sustain it. Much better than adorning the plate of some
hipster diner at the new trendy sushi bar, where I would
perhaps be mentioned in passing in a Yelp review.

Its fur will be warm, its desire for me pure, its need
elemental. It will love me. And so, I make my way towards
its fleeting embrace. The way will be long, often torturous
and pain-laden. But there will occasionally be birdsong. And
the trilling of humanity. So I will try not to hurry.

And along the way, I shall tell jokes.

Literary Analysis

The best thing
about poems
about elevators
is that they work
on every level.

Icon

He's there every morning.
In the vanguard silhouetted,
hacky-sacking in the parking lot corner
as I drive by on the way to work.

Every morning,
sheen of sun off a shaved head.
Passed from foot to foot
the flaccid sack kept in play.

Every morning.
As Italy collapses.
As bodies are taken from nursing homes.
As New York is overwhelmed.

Every morning.
Focused, steady, at peace.
Never letting the bean-filled bag hit the ground.
Sharing his grace until we can re-collect our own.

Every morning.
As much a part of a benediction
as the purple-orange glints of sunrise,
and the warbling song of birds.

Rideshare

Before I checked the right lane, a quick head-jerk to be sure I
could safely merge, I really didn't pay much attention to you,
Sohu. You were just my fourteenth rider that day. Nothing
but human white noise. Noted, but not processed.

But when you started at my sudden movement, I felt the fear.
Hiding in eyes behind a mauve *hijab*, the look the gazelle
gives the crocodile, weighing the personal significance of
appetite. The awareness that you became a kinetic statistic
the moment you got in the car (yet, how miraculous and
divine that you got in anyway?); eyes that accept the next
choice, the one that determines the outcome of this Hadron
collision, is mine to make.

Names are like recycled plastic bags, skin suits stretched
thin, into which we've been poured.
But all names come from somewhere. Mean something. Your
name means "star," or "princess" in Urdu. My name derives
from the Latin word for "small." My surname, incidentally, is
Hungarian for "shepherd" (So you can think of me as the
"Little Shepherd" if you like, Sohu, if that assuages your
fear).

Of course, the idea that I could be threatening or dangerous is
absurd. To me. And which me is it you fear? Is it my
whiteness? My maleness? My size, strength, age? Or perhaps
an assumed Christianity that has branded your *hijab*
suspicious? You are right to fear all of these me's, Sohu. For
I am all of them. I am your lover; I am your killer; I am the
older brother and the fleeting stranger. The one you never
want to see again; the one you look longingly for
everywhere. And I'm everyone and everything in between.
As are you.

What favorite songs do we share? What movies have we
never seen? Are you my familiar, Sohu? Or I, your gargoyle?
Are we cosmic detritus floating on an ether of our own
crafting, placidly tornadic? In what corners of my mind will
you echo; in what nightmares shall I linger, both of us
pondering the unbridgability of chasms, or the possible
beauty of surging rivers, miraculously forded.

Staycation

Years ago, I spent two weeks at Great Smoky Mountain
National Park, so I know that at dusk elk herds will waft into
the meadows of Cataloochee; that even in good weather, fog
and clouds will shroud Clingman's Dome. I can smell the
sun-showered grass along the trails of Balsam Mountain,
hear the thunder claps marking my hike with punctuated
applause, and the trill of Abrams Creek behind my tent.

Last year, I visited the Yellowstone, so I know that wolf
packs still fly across the Lamar Valley, that a thickness of
bison can make the road along Specimen Ridge impassable,
can still feel the titillating fear of the grizzly miles from the
trailhead parking lot as we hike toward Wraith Falls, still feel
primordial awe at the calderas pocketing Artists Paintpots.

But this year's trip to Canyonlands will not happen, caught in
the ripple of pandemic, so I have only pictures in a
guidebook and a penciled-out itinerary; know only that
silence echoes along the red rock. But sometimes, I can
almost hear the call of a lone hawk, vectoring along currents
above the park's north mesa, can almost smell juniper and
pinyon pine on the wind whipping among the plinths and
spires of the Needles, can almost believe that such places still
exist.

The Once and Future King

When the loneliness gets codified, you learn to redefine pleasures. Evenings Hulu-ed. Silicone intimacies. Surrogated body pillows, fabric softener perfumed. Recipes that serve 4-6 serve one all week, until another recipe comes in for its monthly shift. Invented ceremonies that fool no one (for there is no one left to fool). The shame of reading glasses a wasted vanity. This, the status newly quo-ed.

When the loneliness gets codified, friends call from time to time from their paired platforms with ambassadorial check-ins (which is very nice). They do not know the echo of the one-bedroom apartment, the ghost of daily plans, thin-lined coffee pots that promise only a second cup, the indeterminate laughter of a chalk-outlined future.

When the loneliness gets codified, you no longer look into the opacity of forward, you forget the feeling of being touched, and you worry; worry of sunsets unshared, worry that solitary habits calcify, worry that something, and that something else.

When the loneliness gets codified, you wonder about that incorrigible stirring that lingers long after it has any reason to linger, the flicker of an anarchy that was once and still very much is

you.

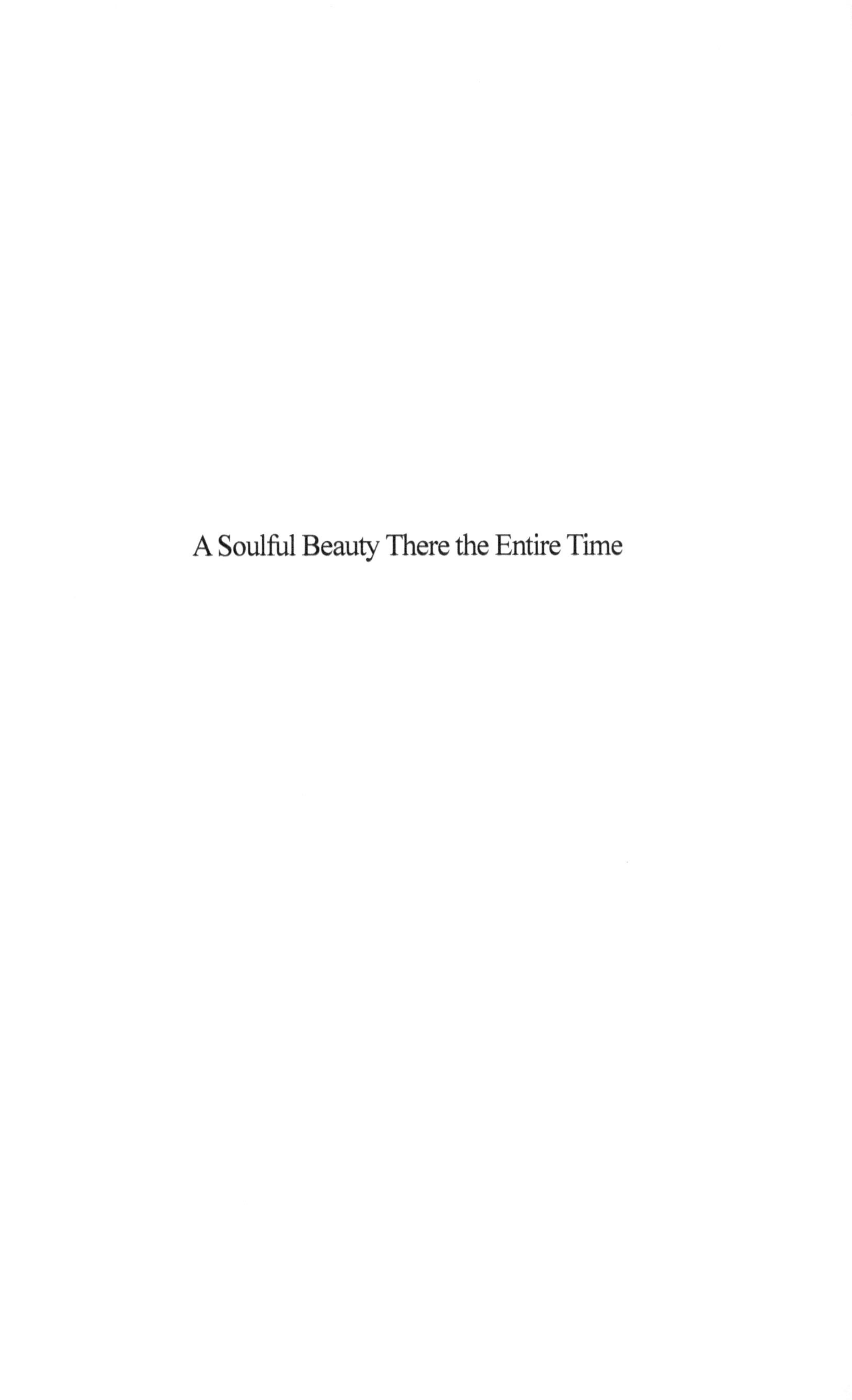

A Soulful Beauty There the Entire Time

Lifeguard

Sometimes I like to pretend the body pillow is you, pulling it close and snug against my body, giving it my warmth. In this wish dream, you give yours back. My arm snakes above your hip, over your stomach, up through the valley. In your half-sleep haze, you understand this is not a request for what came before and what may come later, that this is about why those things come. In your half-sleep haze, you grasp the promise of connection, resting your hand on my forearm, tethering me after so much time adrift, telling me I am no longer drowning. Although I still am. As are you, in your half-sleep haze.

Snowstorm in Oklahoma

As a boy in Connecticut, snowstorms were a commonplace, taken for granted. With the surface satisfaction of youth, I focused on the things that attended—snowball fights, school closings, sledding—the value of the thing itself stayed cloaked and unheeded.

As an adult in Pennsylvania, I exchanged the old irrelevancies for new, complaining of the things that attended—shoveling driveways, sketchy commutes, delays of desired things— in the rush to gild myself with accomplishment external.

Today, a world muted in early-morning purity offers no other terms than its own, calling me out to the balcony, a cup of black coffee warming my hands, to sit and watch a levelling of lawns in powdery sameness, to sit and listen to deep, patient silence.

Morning Moon

There's something soothing
about a moon
that lingers
in the cold morning air,
hanging in the cloudless
blue-screen palimpsest sky;

something that undercuts
the tyranny of time—
that hamster wheel we buy
for ourselves;
something that whispers the liminal,
where I do not have to choose, do not have to
accept the childish construct
of either/or.

Talisman

I have a talisman. I carry it in my pocket. It was given to me last year by a blind man, for what he called "my kindness," which was nothing more than an Uber ride home, because I thought the early dark of December relevant. He described the tree in his front yard with such precision, such memorized detail, I had no need to strain for the house number, flaked in faded paint on the curb. For this, he gave me the talisman. A large bronze-colored coin, eagle on one side, thumb worn human form draped in a flowing gown on the other. "It has no monetary value," the blind man told me, "but it will bring you good luck."

I've carried it in my pocket for almost a full year now. In that span of time, I have found, instead of fame and wealth, unemployment. I am still single (although my ex-wife is not). My hair greys at the temple and chin, my body wakes with aches of age. I often think of driving to Lake Hefner and tossing my talisman far into its ochre depths. But then I remember that my car has a flat tire and the registration has expired. And I'd probably throw out my shoulder. I wish the blind man had just given me cash.

I've carried it in my pocket for almost a full year now. In that span of time, no drunk drivers have T-boned me on their blurred and slurred way home; there have been no in-home invasions, no TVs stuck on FoxNews, I have not found my way into new toxic relationships or haphazardly-designed corn mazes. I have not been crushed by a tree limb, by trickle-down-economics or by a two-ton heavy thing. I have not been mauled by a bear, or a tiger, or a glyptodont. I have not been diagnosed with cancer or (if cancer seems overly-dramatic) with syphilis. The roof does not leak. I have not been arrested. I have not vomited. The house plant a friend

gave me as an apartment-warming present is—
miraculously—still alive.

I have a talisman. I carry it in my pocket. It has no monetary
value. On the rare occasions that I forget it on my nightstand,
I feel naked and unbalanced, for I have grown accustomed to
its weight.

Returning to Carlsbad Caverns, Post-Divorce

Two and a half decades ago, she stopped us somewhere along this trail, pointed at some striking formation of soda-straw and speleothem, fluorescently-backlit curtesy of the NPS, and offered a promise, "whichever of us dies first will wait for the other's soul here." There was something practiced about the declaration, a hollow Hallmark Channel formality. But after two hours of hiking behind those thighs, the rounded curves of her backside, there's not much I wouldn't have agreed to. 750 feet underground, the idea of whim seemed as distant as surface light.

And now here I am again, returning to a favorite place favorite long before her. My hand sliding along the cold, slick handrail as I wind a path along the walkwayed-edges of the Big Room, as awe-struck by the subterranean grandeur as I've ever been, full of the wonderment of the inexorable surrounding, almost hearing the faded echoes of stone laughing at the things we think eternal, I think about the spot, a negative for a photo never developed, afterimage of a life calcified.

I finish the loop without finding it, briefly contemplate a second go-around to satisfy a lingering curiosity, before deciding to head to the elevators instead. We indulge so many whims in a lifetime, why add one more? As I rise to meet the ground, sun and cloud, the things of the surface, questions—perhaps idle ones— remain:

where, unfettered by broken vows, will my soul go now?
And who will be waiting for me when I get there?

Walking Stick

Found it when I was seventeen, camping with a half-dozen buddies the summer before our senior year. A perfectly-shaped piece of dead wood. I gave it a name—Gollum, who, despite his many rather obvious character flaws, was certainly an accomplished hiker—and carved a Janus head for a handle.

I don't know what kind of tree it came from. Red maple, maybe. I don't know much about such things. It's shared some of my best moments for thirty-three years now. Found a small waterfall nestled near the Cataloochee meadows in the Great Smokeys, cleared back ocotillo from a path near the cavern's mouth in Carlsbad, heard elk bugles echo in the dusk of the Yellowstone; faced the wind atop Texas's Guadalupe, caught the sun's earliest rays on top of Maine's Cadillac.

Much of its bark has flaked off over the years. Three decades of skin oil and sweat has massaged the back half of the Janus face smooth. While it may look old, fragile, and weathered, surely some fulgent and unyielding wonders await it still.

Creative Differences

She kept the Nagel, even though I bought it a few years before we were together. Still, it seemed right; she was the horse person. I simply bought it because I liked the colors, had never seen a purple horse. And now probably never will.

But what I still find galling is that even though we agreed I'd keep it, she decided at the last moment that Parkes's "Gargoyles" would stay. She had always hated the Parkes, but now wouldn't let it go, because she liked how it matched the paint in the hallway. I didn't want to make a scene in front of the kids, but that one stung. I loved that painting; the soft side of darkness, the desire of monsters to not just protect innocence, but to, upon occasion, break character and play with it. I had always wanted such a gargoyle. Now I probably won't find one.

She also said I could have Munch's "The Scream," but in the month between when I moved out and came back later for the rest of my things, it seems to have disappeared. My kids swear that it's not on any of the walls in her possession, nor will it ever apparently hang on those in mine.

The only artwork she willingly gave up was the one of seven dogs playing poker (officially titled "A Friend in Need"). She truly *hated* that one. Found it tacky, uncouth, and without substance. And it didn't even match any paint in the house. She either couldn't see or didn't appreciate the painting's subtleties. That the bulldog is cheating, slipping the ace of clubs to his friend on the left. That the Doberman in the right corner notices but smokes his pipe in silent acquiescence. And that the dog being helped not only had the biggest stack of chips at the table, but was already holding all of the aces.

Poetry on the Balcony

I like to start my day with some black coffee and poetry on the balcony. I've tried to read inside, but it's not the same; it's missing a soundtrack I have come to enjoy, perhaps even need.

I go out each morning after the morning commute has cleared the parking lot, so this soundtrack is mostly inhuman: a tremulant Oklahoma wind, the cadence of late autumn rain, and one morning this past December, the absorbing silence of snowfall.

And then there's the birds. Crows cawing out odes. Doves, mixing their cliched cooing with another call, a jarring, unworldly caw of their own, untimbred with the wise malice of the crow. The rest of the birds I can't identify. That academic knowledge has long since slipped by. I no longer mourn its passage, opting instead to simply accept these true notes of beauty as the world's proper legacy.

But today, I'm having a hard time concentrating, having difficulty moving through T.S. Eliot. Not because of any difficulty with the lines or an opacity of image, but because my typical inhuman soundtrack is, this morning, decidedly human. Some chucklehead is sitting in his car, waiting for someone, while a catastrophic bass thumps the world. I can't access what song is being listened to, I can't even be sure there *is* a song. All the world is this constant, throbbing, bass.

Thump.
Thump.
Thump.

While I read:

"We are the hollow men.
We are the stuffed men."

Thump.
Thump.
Thump.

While I wonder if I am right to hear echoes of Yeats in the
lines:

"And voices are
In the wind's singing
More distant and more solemn
Than a fading star."

Thump.
Thump.
Thump.

While I try to understand Eliot's Shadow, and where it falls.

Thump.
Thump.
Thump.

It's disturbing, discordant. It frustrates me. It scares off the
birds, drowns out the wind, virtually erases Eliot.

And it makes me worry. I worry that my hold on poetry (or at
least on Eliot) is so tenuous that this mundanity sunders.

I worry that this bass is so thunderous, so orbit-altering, that
it will shake the world free of its mooring and it will float
untethered.

And I worry that, despite my frustration, the near-certainty
that within moments I will give up Eliot as a lost cause,

despite all of my profound annoyance at this bass thumping,
my foot taps along to its pulse.

-85-

Circle of Stones

1.

They'll gather around the circle of stones tonight, as they did
the night before, and the night before that. Drinking their
Scotch and swapping stories of hunts past, like when Uncle
John once shot a buck from the outhouse seat. Only, the first
shot did not bring the deer down, so he had to waddle out of
the shithouse, pants around his ankles, toilet paper flapping
behind him like a tail, to squeeze off the killing shot. They'll
all laugh, then break out the *szalona.* As the grease-heavy
slab hisses into the fire, they'll mock first wives, second
wives, third. Eventually, one will ask me how it was possible
I didn't see any deer today. They'll laugh and joke about how
bad I am at this. They'll think my smile shows I'm one of
them.

2.

I heard the doe before I saw her. Labored, panicked
breathing; the thrashing of her wounded thigh muffled by the
leaf-litter; sounds folding into the liminal of an afternoon
nap. She lay nestled on the other side of the perpendiculared
logs against which I rested, fearful eyes locked on mine. One
of them will be here soon, looking to finish her off, so I let
the details permeate: The way her breath-steam floats,
joining the smaller cloud of heat escaping from the wound on
her thigh; that a timeless fern fans behind one ear, like she's
wearing a flower in her hair; that fear has fled those liquid-
amber eyes, defiant now, as if asking me about a soul.
Slowly, unfolding the hours within the minutes, I crawl to her
side. There's blood, but not much. If they don't find her,
she'll be fine. Shadows stretch themselves across the junction
of hand upon thigh. We lie together, breathing synchronous,
erasing each other until, at the sound of approaching bootfall,

the spell breaks. She bounds through the thorn-choked underbrush, into the verdant beyond, where they can never follow.

3.

They talk of stalks, of ambushes, of blood-drinking, of field-dressings and undressings, as they did the night before, and the night before that. They boast about kills made and side-scores. They tease about kills missed and ex-wives. They make jokes about land-oysters. They think my smile shows I'm one of them. I plan to sit with them for a while, for the transitory warmth of the fire. When it gets too cold, I'll go brave the wall of thorns, breath synchronous in the verdant that lies beyond. While they sit in their circle of stones.

Busk

Thoreau speaks of it in *Walden*,
how the Mucclasse Indians held
an annual busk,
a ritual burning of all that
is worn-out, unneeded, or
weighted with the baggage of life;
a civic bonfire,
and a collective rebirth,
all grievances,
any wrongdoing
short of murder,
forgiven.

Nature approves,
everywhere gives its model.
Winter's winds exfoliate
in advance of April rain;
Snakes slough skin;
birds molt faded feathers;
Moths emerge from
silken sanctuary transformed,
while under raging salt-waves,
the hermit swaps shells
in expansive tranquility.

I drive west, aiming
for a horizon unbridled.
Each mile of Interstate
a purge of expectations
unmade in my image,
ex-life bleached
in my rearview;

up ahead, the highway sign
welcoming me to Oklahoma,
and to the ceremony
of First-Fruits that lies beyond.

Ceremony

For a soundtrack, I try for something expansive to drown out
Anderson Cooper's reporting and the all-too expert analysis
of Drs. Gupta and Fauci, but also something appropriately
circumstantial, the right blend of looming menace and
uplifting hope. I select Greig's "In the Hall of the Mountain
King," and begin.

I use a razor blade for the garlic. I want it so thin it liquesces
into the butter in perfect embrace.

I do the onions next; bending my fingers palmward,
presenting knuckles only to the blade's smirk. I blink at the
pungency and slice translucent.

The two plum tomatoes I scavenged from the panic-
plundered bins at Wal-Mart are not perfect, but they'll do,
rinsed and diced and patient in a stainless-steel bowl next to
the range.

The basil sits in a cup of water, clinging to life just a little
while longer.

The chicken breast, coated in a mix of panko and parmesan,
waits in the cold dark of the refrigerator.

The butter and garlic blended symbiotic, I unroll the chicken
tenderly into the pan. A hiss of protest unzippers the kitchen
with hints of sage, a promise of oregano. Five minutes per
side, then the taut goldenness removed to the oven while I
make the sauce.

A splash of wine to deglaze, morsels of meat loosened from
the pan's plain. More butter, with the onions in tow. The
tomatoes join the dance shortly after. When they've given up

their liquid, I'll add the cream. The transubstantiation of basil comes last.

I take time with the presentation. The plate undersauced, I lay a bias-cut chicken half horizontally across, its partner angled on edge, a promise pointing skyward. Additional sauce drizzled over the whole, the rest reserved in a bowl in case of need. Two last leaves of basil, held in reserve, now draped across *in memoriam*.

I pour a glass of *Marqués de Cáceres* Crianza 2014, breathing the while at the counter corner, and I sit down to a dinner for one.

I Hiked Alone (Mostly)

The first mile into the Wichita fills itself with mundane
concern. The complaint of knee, selected socks too thick,
distribution of pack-weight evaluated, re-evaluated. These
things soon left behind, pushed aside by the vibrancy of the
occasional wildflower, stubborn and hardy: mirroring blues,
red, like fresh blood, a yellow so impossibly yellow it seems
fake, and whites so white they sting the eye with glare.

I let an older couple pass, briefly envying their
companionship until they horizon and fade, then
I resume my fierce solitude, scurrying up, passing through,
sliding down red rock, prickly pear, and scrub grass. I give a
passing thought to mountain lions, wonder what they are
called around here: puma, cougar, panther?

A few hours in, the high sun splashes down, sending a warm
chill through me, an embrace that could pass for love. I'll
regret the lack of sunscreen, or a hat to cover the unfallow
oval of scalp no length of hair tendrils over, but not yet.

This will be what post-apocalyptic wandering will be like,
which makes the day good practice. A rehearsal but also a
repetition. I used to hike alone, then with a wife, then a
family, now alone again. I enjoy it mostly, and I pay no mind
to the vulture that follows in my wake.

Pinnacle

Somewhere between miles 14 and 15 the panic set in. Tight switchbacks, no guardrails, low-geared descending cars insisting on lane integrity. With no one to share the driving, I gave up sneaking glances at the vistas the pamphlet said reached to New Mexico, Kansas, Oklahoma, and Wyoming by mile 10. Consumed by fear, worried that with the steepness of the slant, the car will flip over backwards, I grip the wheel, body rigid, eyes locked before me, mumbling curses at Zebulon Pike.

I can't see the curve for the next switchback. Instead, it seems like the road is a ramp, ready to launch the car into the impossibly-blue before me. Of course, at this crawling speed, there would be no liftoff, just an uninspiring trickle, a rolling crinkle of metal, a bounding downslope full of pain, terror, and death.

And that's when I see them. Septuagenarians sitting on the tailgate of a truck pointed downslope, her arm snaked across his back, his holding her shoulder snug. The embrace confident, deserved, devoid of the desperation of youth. Isolated amongst the multitude, they sit, gazing east, a unity earned and inviolate.

A slice of their peace stays with me, helps me around the next few bends, but its potency wanes, is gone by mile 16, and I turn around, still three miles from the summit. Not cowardice, I tell myself. Just saving it for another day.

When I see the couple again, I smile, sensing that someday their shared serenity will be mine and a yet-unknown hers.

But I also think about ramming their truck with my car, pushing them over the side.

Because they just seemed so damned happy.
-94-

Thanksgiving

"The question is not what you look at, but what you see."
                                    Henry David Thoreau

What would Thoreau say to the friend for whom I pet sat,
who returned home from a long weekend getaway and
grumbled of dog hair on the couch and the need to re-order
from Farmer's Dog so soon?

Or to my mother, who diminished my last Christmas gift by
noting she is not a fan of Rioja, nor claret, prefers a Carlos
Rossi Chablis?

What would Thoreau say to the man in the custom-tailored
suit in Delmonico's, complaining his steak is undercooked?
Or to the hiker dismayed that the trail is poorly marked?

I think of Henry—and of the multitudes surrounding, for
whom gifts are not gifty enough—this morning as I squint
through my commute, these engulfing rays, this enfolding
warmth, my motion more an act of faith than intentional
progress. I think of Henry, and refuse to reach for sunglasses.

She Received a Mysterious Plant

She received a mysterious plant. Everything about it was mysterious. The pot granular, sugary like Kool-Aid; a faded tuscon decored with pale blue cabalistic images, hieroglyphics reading "Anfractuous," although she never knew this, not speaking plant. When she watered the plant—a full cup every week—as the dream directed her, the pot liquified, flowed away, exposing the rounded trapezoid of soil. And about that soil: flaked feldspar interspersed with what looked like the novelty gum nuggets sold in small burlap sacks in vintage candy shoppes, could very well be the novelty gum nuggets sold in small burlap sacks in vintage candy shoppes (for she never had the nerve to taste it). The plant itself a tattered assemblage of leftover parts. Some leaves, some succulent spines, a little evergreen. She thought spruce, maybe juniper, but she did not know much about such things. There were flowers, berries, cones, other arboreal accessories as yet unidentifiable. It was a mess, really. A collage of cast-off pieces. And did I mention the shimmering? The plant shimmered. Sometimes it looked to her like it was dancing. Other times it vanished completely, did an invisible lap around the room and reappeared almost—but not quite—in the exact spot from which it left. Such a mysterious plant. Everything about it was mysterious. Even who sent it to her.

But sometimes, if she squinted just a bit, and caught the plant in just the right light, it looked like everything she always wanted.

Doppelgänger

The letter was strange, wondrous. The Dean of Students, in a tone somehow both firm and avuncular, chastened me for poor class attendance. He also expressed some concern that I had not yet checked into my room at Morgan Hall, nor activated my OWLcard, which I gathered from context was connected to the university's meal plan. This was a most ill-advised start to my freshman year, the Dean suggested, not in keeping with the Owl way. He closed the letter with his best wishes and fervent hopes that my studies at Temple University would be lauded and enriching. A letter most strange indeed, as I was months deep into my studies at the University of Illinois, in Champaign-Urbana, a smallish college town sieged by cornfields approximately 762 miles away from Philadelphia, when I received it.

When I applied to Temple and never heard back, I headed west, leaving a shadow behind, an outline that, apparently, Temple was expecting. I often think of this me, who had been assigned a dorm room, an OWLcard, a student ID; who somehow recorded a first semester GPA (0.2, as a more stern follow-up letter from the Dean informed me). I wonder if he enjoyed living in Philadelphia, as I would have done? Did he definitively decide between Geno's and Pat's (the answer is Pat's, of course)? Did he sometimes roll an ankle on the uneven cobblestones of Elfreth's Alley? Place pennies on Franklin's gravestone? Watch the Delaware's moonlight wink under the Whitman Bridge?

Does this version of me play golf? Or go to his high school reunions? Does he still have a wife? Does he still talk to his father? Does he take dutiful vacations? Is shame beneath his paygrade? Does he say words like "bungalow" without irony? Believe in divining rods? Has he achieved what a

Dean of Students would consider "success?" And has that translated into happiness?

Would he find the idea of me as interesting as I find the idea of him? Would he be surprised to find me living in Oklahoma, writing poetry? Would he marvel at my helter-skelter journey? If we were to meet, would we recognize which the intended path, who the evil twin?

And would the recognition matter?

Traffic Light Gaze

She slides alongside me in the left-turn lane. It's past dusk, so I can't tell whether her dress, adorned with bright sunflowers, is black or dark blue. She is radiant with echoes of atmosphere I've known only in dream, the tug of a lost puzzle piece, the whispered word completing a struggled-over line of poetry.

In the blink of a shared, red-glared moment years unfold:

Our first date will be lunch at a bistro table beside Lake Hefner. When a seagull steals a chip she drops, we laugh, and recognize this is the thing we'll work up into a story years from now when friends ask us when we knew. In the early days, we go hiking, tell each other stories, read each other poems. The first time we make love, it will be awkward in all the ways you want it to be awkward, the ways that tell you one day soon the awkwardness will cocoon into synchrony. We'll have a fight about moving in together, about who moves where, like arguing, we soon realize, about which ocean is wetter. We laugh at our folly, and then go out for sushi, splitting a rainbow roll (as has become our custom). After dinner we go adopt a dog. We discover in each other a balm for the pre-us wounds that never heal, but, we learn, can fade. We get married in a church because it's important to her mother, but the guest list is small, for the ceremony was completed long ago at, of all places, a traffic light. In the last days, we go hiking, tell each other stories, read each other poems.

The shared red-glare vanishes. She gets the arrow and turns. I move forward towards the next intersection.

Flight

He watches the seemingly-endless stream pour into night,
disgorged from the maw of the cavern, his face wrapped in
wonderment.

For nearly twenty minutes, we watch the millions stream
unvectored into the dimming New Mexico sky, a stream of
life flowing and eternal, unhampered and unconcerned about
an owl stalking the fringes, plucking a single victim,
returning to perch on a shadowy cactus arm, returning a short
while later to pluck another.

My son sits on the hard stone and concrete amphitheater
before the cavern entrance, unhampered and unconcerned,
rapt in delight and marvel. The park ranger's presentation has
long since echoed away, most of the spectators have grown
weary and Nature-sated, shuffling up the aisles towards the
next guide-book mandate.

But we stay. Until the sky-flood of bats slows to a steady
trickle. We stay, until after the owl is sated and shuffles off to
wherever sated owls shuffle. We stay, until the last of the
light fades.

And then we stay beyond.

Soundtrack for a Pandemic

This morning, I select Faith No More's "Epic."

There is no prelude. The song just explodes. To call it
cacophony would be kindness.
Lead vocals confuse. Is this rap? Grunge? Both? Neither?
The chorus unravels, circles back on itself. Existential
questions jutting up against nihilism.
The musical structure is inverted, the percussion taking the
forefront, bass and electric guitar as backdrop. Until it
switches. Then switches back. A kaleidoscopic musical
fever-dream.

And then, as the drums and the guitars and Mike Patton's
yawping subside, fading away into echoes, you hear it: the
piano. Dripping like a slow, steady rain. A soulful beauty
there the entire time.

The Last Poem in a Collection

There are things we expect from the last poem in a collection.
We expect some form of closure. We want a circle
completed, a character arc finished. We want a poem that
points outward, offers some thoughts on where we go from
here. If the collection has been a journey, we want to be
there, wherever the "there" may be, whatever the "there"
may represent. If the collection has been dark, we want some
light, some reason to feel that Happiness writ large is still
possible, for us, for the poet, for everyone.

But there are times when it is hard for the poet, for the comic,
to satisfy expectations. Bill Hicks would sometimes go off
the rails during his act, leaving the jokes behind, giving voice
to the dark poetry within, unsettling the audience.
Sometimes, he would sense the looming disconnect, a key
and lock not quite fitting, and would speak to expectations
unmet: assure them: "Hold on. There are dick jokes coming."
The crowd would laugh the realignment.

But there is a cost for laughter. The comic pays it for us all.
He does not want laurels; he does not ask thanks. All he
wants is for you to keep laughing. For the same reasons he
cries his emptiness to sleep, the same reason he toasts his
loneliness on a small balcony. There is a cost, a price he is
more than willing to pay, because your laughter beats back
the dark fire, drowns out the whispers. For a while.

Within the pauses, within the interstices, if the blackness, the
inner life of the comic, grabs the microphone for a while, be
patient, and know there will be dick jokes soon.

Resting in That Beat Between Breaths

Exhale

I'm up earlier than normal.
Sit out on the balcony with a cup of coffee—black, like my
soul, I'd Dad joke to my sons if they were around to groan.

How close the silence this morning is.
A light breeze tousles the tree across the way,
A squirrel soliloquy from a partially-hidden branch.
A faint susurrus of car noise muffled by distance,
But little else.
Even the accustomed bird song is absent, as if my early
arrival has caught them unaware and unprepared.
But silence is a shallow and paltry word. This is something
else, the world resting in that beat between breaths.

Wasted vapor bleeds from mug into cold autumn air
as I sit weighing pressures, chasing thoughts, half-dreading
the confusion that attends catching one.

A single dove lands on the balcony railing, not even two feet
away from where I sit. Struck by such willful proximity, I sit
as still as the morning sounds.
There is communion here. A solemn solidarity. I sense that
much. But its import eludes me.
If he asked me for a dollar, I would give it to him, although I
would not know where to find it.
If he asked me where his mate was, I'd help him search,
although I do not know what she looks like.
He side-eyes my stillness for a while, as if expecting
something, then flies off to the horizon. I long to mimic his
alien movement, to explain myself.

Were these just random vectors colliding one early autumn
morning, sharing a space and a time? Or was this Keats's
Nightingale, Hardy's Thrush, Whitman's Mockingbird? If so,

what was the pedagogy? And if I fail to catch it will the dove
return to try again? How many bites of the apple does one
get?

Or perhaps the dove wasn't the teacher, but the lesson.
Maybe the morning wasn't instructive, but instruction.

I go back inside, make a second pot of coffee and return to
the balcony.
There is birdnoise once again,
The morning has caught up.
The parking lot below fulsome with the controlled chaos of
neighbors piling into cars, rushing off to the confines of their
Sunday worship.

The sunrise now well behind me, I breathe in the day.

Acknowledgements

With gratitude to the editors of the journals and anthologies where the following poems first appeared:

Tejascovido: "And Now, A Word from Our Sponsors," "Ceremony," "Icon,"

Windward Review: "Staycation."

The Langdon Review of the Arts in Texas: "Icon."

Insurrection: "Support Group"

The Oklahoma Review: "Et in Arcadia, Ego," "Most Wanted," and "She Received a Mysterious Plant."

Jerry Jazz Musician: "Coltrane."

About the Author

Living what could charitably be called a nomadic life, Paul Juhasz was born in western New Jersey, grew up just outside New Haven, Connecticut, and has spent appreciable chunks of his life in the plains of central Illinois, in the upper hill country of Texas, and in the Lehigh Valley in Pennsylvania. Most recently seduced by the spirit of the red earth, he now lives in Oklahoma City. A graduate of the Red Earth M.F.A., his work has appeared in several literary journals, most recently *Concho River Review*, *Poetry Quarterly*, *Oklahoma Review*, and *Main Street Rag*. He has served a s director of the Woody Guthrie Poets from 2020-2022. His first book, *Fulfillment: Diary of a Warehouse Picker*—a mock journal covering his six-month stint in an Amazon warehouse—was published by Fine Dog Press in 2020. His second book, *Ronin*, a collection of (mostly) prose poems—also published by Fine Dog Press—was named a finalist for the 2022 Oklahoma Book Award in poetry.